Pictures from the Bible 1

Emil Maier-F.

The Loving Father

with a storytelling aid
by Magdalena Spiegel

Abingdon Press
Nashville

ISBN 0-687-22819-0

The Loving Father

Translation copyright © 1983 by Abingdon Press

Originally published as *Vom verzeihenden Vater*

© 1978 Verlag Katholisches Bibelwerk GmbH, Stuttgart
as ISBN 3-460-24011-3

The scripture passages are from the Revised Standard Common Bible,
copyright © 1973 by the National Council of Churches of Christ,
and are used by permission.

Printed in Italy by A. Mondadori Verona

There was a man who had two sons.

"I want to go away from home," said the younger son to his father.

"Give me the money that will belong to me, after you are dead."

The father gave him the money.
Sadly he watched his son,
as he left home.

The younger son went to a big city
where he could live as he pleased.

He had money, and soon
he had many friends.
But the friends only
wanted his money.

One day he said to his friends,
"I don't have any more money."
Then they left him.

He became poor and lonely.

He was hungry.
No one gave him
anything to eat.

Finally he
begged a farmer,

"Let me take care of
your pigs!"

He took care
of the pigs.

He even ate
the pigs' food.

It tasted awful.
He was still hungry.

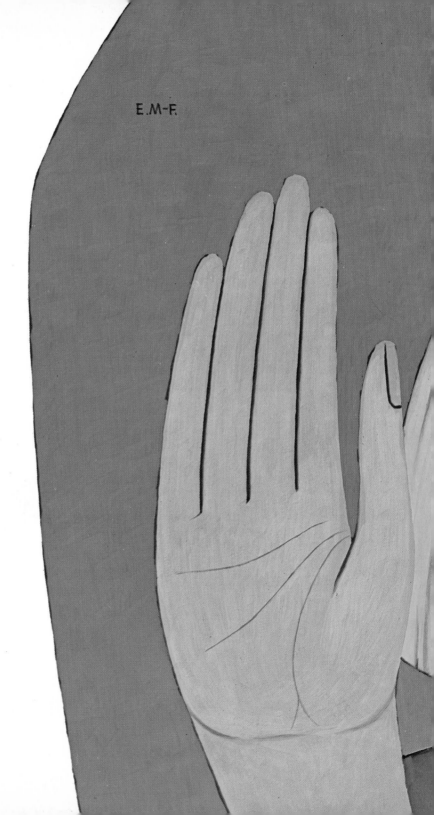

He thought,
If I could only work
for my father,
I would have
enough to eat.

I will go home and
tell my father
just how badly
I have behaved.

At home his
father waited
every day for his
younger son to return.

When he saw
him coming,
he ran to meet him.

The son
wanted to tell his father
all the things
he had done wrong.

But his father
hugged him and said:

"I'm glad
you are home!"

His father gave him a new coat
and prepared a great feast.
He thought everyone
would be happy
with him.

But the older son,
who had
stayed at home,
did not want to come
to the feast.

Their father went
to him and said,
"I love you just as much
as I love your brother.
Come with me
to the feast, and
be happy with me
that your brother finally
has come home."

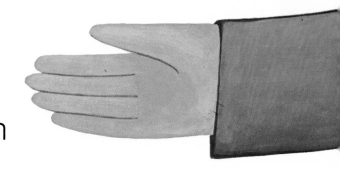

For parents and educators in using this picture book

Before we look at this picture book with our children and tell them the Bible story, we should try to understand the contents and intentions of the book. This is essential. First we read the Bible passage to understand the whole concept of the message. Then let the words sink in, think about them, listen, let them "move in your heart." Only after we find the right approach to this message, can we present it to the children. We can then reach our goal, which is to persuade the children to have faith, love, and hope for present or future situations. Leading the children to the biblical happenings can be done two ways.

One is to tell the children the story first. This way we stay with the text and develop it to the better understanding of the child. By maintaining eye contact with the child, we can sense difficulty in understanding and can resolve it by repeating or expanding the text without adding a moralistic psychological meaning. The children listen to the story, their imagination and creativity will be stimulated, and they will picture the story. Only then should the pictures in the book be looked at, recognized, and the story related. Later the short text can be read, or the child may read the text for themselves.

A second possibility is to begin with the book. The pictures are shown as motivation. The children react spontaneously to it, express their feelings, which can be encouraged by parents or teachers. Let the children find out by themselves as much as possible.

Then the text of the picture book can be used and discussed. One can also freely explain without using the text. With both methods, the telling and looking at the pictures should not end the story. Discussions, drawings, playing different parts, singing, or a prayer can reinforce what the children heard and saw, and bring it closer to their own lives.

The parable of the loving father
Luke 15:11-32

[11]And he said, "There was a man who had two sons; [12]and the younger of them said to his father, 'Father, give me the share of property that falls to me.' And he divided his living between them. [13]Not many days later, the younger son gathered all he had and took his journey into a far country, and there he squandered his property in loose living. [14]And when he had spent everything, a great famine arose in that country, and he began to be in want. [15]So he went and joined himself to one of the citizens of that country, who sent him into his fields to feed swine. [16]And he would gladly have fed on the pods that the swine ate; and no one gave him anything. [17]But when he came to himself he said, 'How many of my father's hired servants have bread enough and to spare, but I perish here with hunger! [18]I will arise and go to my father, and I will say to him, "Father, I have sinned against heaven and before you; [19]I am no longer worthy to be called your son; treat me as one of your hired servants." ' [20]And he arose and came to his father. But while he was yet at a distance, his father saw him and had compassion, and ran and embraced him and kissed him. [21]And the son said to him, 'Father, I have sinned against heaven and before you; I am no longer worthy to be called your son.' [22]But the father said to his servants, 'Bring quickly the best robe, and put it on him; and put a ring on his hand, and shoes on his feet; [23]and bring the fatted calf and kill it, and let us eat and make merry; [24]for this my son was dead, and is alive again; he was lost, and is found.' And they began to make merry.

[25] "Now his elder son was in the field; and as he came and drew near to the house, he heard music and dancing. [26]And he called one of the servants and asked what this meant. [27] And he said to him, 'Your brother has come, and your father has killed the fat-

ted calf, because he has received him safe and sound.' ²⁸But he was angry and refused to go in. His father came out and entreated him, ²⁹but he answered his father, 'Lo, these many years I have served you, and I never disobeyed your command; yet you never gave me a kid, that I might make merry with my friends. ³⁰But when this son of yours came, who has devoured your living with harlots, you killed for him the fatted calf!' ³¹And he said to him, 'Son, you are always with me, and all that is mine is yours. ³²It was fitting to make merry and be glad, for this your brother was dead, and is alive; he was lost, and is found.' "

What is the story all about?

To the indignation of the scribes and Pharisees Jesus welcomed sinners and took meals with them. Jesus answered the objections in the parables of the lost: the lost sheep, the lost coin, and the lost son. These parables deal with something fundamental about the kingdom of God. The parables deal with a different measure of justice. Here we are dealing with the joy of finding. The lost one is received with open arms and sheltered in human love extending from the love of God. The father in this parable is, in his love, an image of God's love. God says yes to failures who return to him. The faith in the mercy of the father determines the understanding for human life, as Jesus said, "This my son was dead, and is alive again."

Which way does the younger son go now?

He demanded from the father the part that was rightfully his according to the Jewish law under which the firstborn received double the share. Thus the later born son received one third. This inheritance would become valid after the death of the father or during his lifetime with the condition that the heir would have ownership, but no right to disposal or profit. Here the son demanded all. He turned everything into money and emigrated. Emigration was not unusual in Palestine because of the better living conditions elsewhere. In the "far country" he squandered his money. He went to a citizen of the country and begged to tend his swine. The Jews thought he was abandoning his beliefs, and he could not celebrate Sabbath because he handled unclean animals. Under the pressure of his distress he realized his guilt, turned around, and went home to his father. He realized that he did not deserve to be his father's son. He wanted to be a servant. But his father ran toward him. He embraced his son and kissed him. He gave him a new cloak, a sign of distinction, and shoes, the sign of a free man. He had a feast prepared and accepted the young man back at his table. These were outward signs of forgiveness and acceptance.

The story however has a second climax. It describes the protest of the older son. This son had proved himself through the years in performance and conduct. He did not understand the feast and his father's actions. He had no desire to call the returned son his brother. The father went to him. The father let him voice his protest and then tried to make it clear that he would not be short-changed. "All that I have is yours. As my son you also have to be a brother again. This feast is necessary, come and rejoice with us. Come and join us."

Are there experiences in the lives of our children where this gospel message might be helpful? Consider the identification of the sons. Our small children already are under achievement pressure. In our society achievement is a measuring device to self-worth. How often do our children have the experience of failure? Children often feel that they fall short of the expectations of parents and teachers, either in the area of achievement or social behavior. This problem can grow larger if one child is compared to another, or feels that the other one is better. The well-meaning saying of the educators: "If you cannot do one thing well, you can do another," helps very little. Here in Jesus' words we find the answer, the help. God takes us in his arms. He accepts us without prior achievement. He also says yes to a failure. He takes us as we are. This acceptance of the father must be explained to the children. Children sometimes feel real or imaginary injustice. They tried so hard, but their effort is not appreciated. When someone else is praised for a small achievement, children have to learn to overcome envy and jealousy and be happy with the others. Just as the father loved both sons, so we are loved by God and accepted into God's family. This trust and faith should be learned by children. A play with different characters would be helpful, to bring this parable to an imagined finish.

We should not hesitate to tell our children this story, even if it is not needed for a particular situation. The typical picture of the good father will be strengthened in the children's minds.

Magdalena Spiegel